The Kemetic Spirituality Workbook for Women

A Practical Guide to Spiritual Evolution Following the Principles of Kemetic Wisdom

Enlightened Editions

TABLE OF CONTENTS

FREE MEDITATIONS

Are you ready to elevate your spiritual journey and unlock the full potential of your inner self?

Deepen your transformation with our free meditations, carefully crafted to enhance and assist you on your spiritual journey.

Meditation 1:
Experience a blissful energetic healing of your heart, reconnecting you with your inner love and radiance, and opening yourself to more abundance in your life.

Meditation 2:
Explore the power of forgiveness with our Forgiveness meditation, where you will be guided through a sacred journey of emotional liberation. Release burdens, cultivate forgiveness, and experience the profound healing that comes from letting go.

Meditation 3:
Connect with your soul with our Higher-self meditation, unlocking inner wisdom, intuition, and spiritual insight.

These meditations, designed to accompany the workbook, serve as potent tools for transformation, healing, and spiritual growth.

Download your FREE meditations by scanning the QR code below:

WELCOME

Welcome to your introductory workbook on Kemetic spirituality—a tailored guide primarily designed for those at the beginning of their spiritual journey. Whether you're new to Kemetic spirituality or seeking a structured exploration of its principles, this workbook, when used with the accompanying book '*Awakening the Sacred Flame: A Beginner's Guide to Kemetic Spirituality*', serves as a foundational step toward understanding and incorporating these ancient teachings into your life.

As you embark on this journey, it may surprise you that much of the exploration is centered on self-discovery rather than a magical journey into ancient Egypt. This shift in focus is intentional, reflecting the true essence of Kemetic spirituality. While ancient Egypt provides the cultural context, at the heart of Kemetic teachings lies alignment with the cosmic order of the universe—an alignment achieved only through deep self-exploration.

This workbook will guide you through key concepts, practices, and reflections that foster self-discovery, growth, and alignment with universal principles. The journey is not about unraveling ancient mysteries—it's about understanding how these teachings can be applied to modern life. It's an invitation to delve into the depths of your being while fostering a harmonious connection with your spiritual path.

As you work your way through these pages, consider how powerful self-exploration can be in aligning yourself with the principles of Ma'at, connecting with your soul, deepening your relationships, connecting with deities, and honoring your ancestral lineage. This approach embraces the idea that the essence of Kemetic spirituality is a continuous journey within, fostering wisdom, balance, and alignment with the divine cosmic order. May this exploration enlighten and transform you, leading towards deeper understanding of both yourself and the sacred teachings of Kemetic spirituality.

WHAT IS KEMETIC SPIRITUALITY?

Kemetic spirituality finds its roots in ancient Egypt, emerging as one of the earliest recorded systems of religious and spiritual customs. Over millennia, it evolved under the influence of unique cultural, social, and metaphysical elements intrinsic to the Nile Valley civilization. Derived from the word 'Kemet,' meaning 'black' or 'dark,' the term 'Kemetic' reflects the fertile black soil of the Nile Delta.

This spiritual tradition was not just a set of beliefs; it was a profound philosophy that intertwined the cosmic with the earthly, bridging the seen with the unseen. Beyond the polytheistic beliefs lay a powerful connection to nature and the divine. Temples, more than mere structures, served as vibrant centers for religious ceremonies, offerings, and festivals.

Integral to Kemetic spirituality were complex funerary practices and a deep-rooted belief in the afterlife. The conviction in the preservation of the soul after death led to elaborate burial rituals, mummification, and the construction of grand tombs and pyramids.

Hieroglyphs, sacred texts, and wisdom literature played a crucial role, conveying spiritual teachings and guiding individuals through the journey of life, death, and the afterlife. Divination methods and dream interpretation were intertwined with daily practices, taught in temples that also served as centers for learning healing arts and sacred text interpretations.

At its core, Kemetic spirituality revolves around Ma'at—the cosmic order that embodies truth, justice, and balance. Ma'at serves as our guide towards personal growth and societal harmony. Although the fall of ancient Egyptian civilization dimmed Kemetic practices, its spiritual legacy persisted. Today, a resurgence of interest in Kemetic spirituality reflects a modern quest for wisdom and connection.

As we embark on this exploration of Kemetic spirituality together, remember that it is more than a historical relic. It offers timeless wisdom, spiritual nourishment, and a profound connection to yourself, to those around you, and to the entire cosmos. Let this workbook be your guide in the sacred dance of Ma'at, where ancient wisdom echoes throughout your spiritual journey.

LIVING IN ALIGNMENT WITH MA'AT

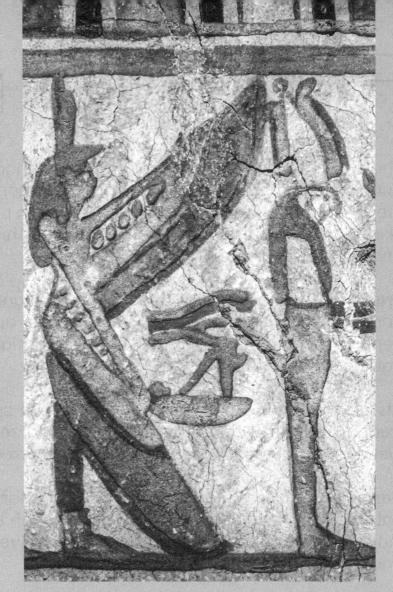

Understanding the principles of Ma'at is crucial to your Kemetic practice. The principles of Ma'at serve as a guiding light to ethical living, as they provide a framework for you to align yourself alongside the cosmic order. By embodying the principles of Ma'at, you have the power to cultivate a balanced, harmonious, and righteous existence.

As a part of Kemetic spirituality, spiritual transformation and personal growth are sought after, with self-reflection and alignment with Ma'at being crucial to doing so. The following questions are intended to inspire deep contemplation and guide personal exploration of the principles of Ma'at in everyday life.

PRINCIPLES OF MA'AT

The ancient Egyptian concept of Ma'at encompasses a set of principles that can guide you toward a harmonious and balanced life. While there are traditionally seven main principles of Ma'at, I like to incorporate two extra principles as this covers a broader understanding. These principles are:

Truth: Upholding truth involves living in alignment with honesty and sincerity, ensuring that your words and actions reflect genuine intentions. It forms the foundation for a just and balanced existence.

Justice: Justice in Ma'at goes beyond legal systems; it involves treating others with fairness, equity, and respect. Striving for justice contributes to a harmonious and ordered society.

Harmony: Harmony emphasizes the importance of maintaining balance and equilibrium in all aspects of life. It encourages individuals to seek balance within themselves, in relationships, and with the natural world.

Order: Order involves organizing and structuring your life in a way that promotes balance and stability. Embracing order contributes to a well-regulated and smoothly functioning existence.

Compassion: Compassion involves extending empathy, kindness, and understanding to others. It encourages you to consider the well-being of others and foster a sense of interconnectedness.

Wisdom: Wisdom is the pursuit of knowledge, self-improvement, and higher truth. It involves cultivating an open mind, critical thinking, and a lifelong commitment to learning.

Reciprocity: Reciprocity emphasizes mutual exchange and interconnectedness. It encourages you to contribute positively to your communities, recognizing that collective well-being is intertwined with personal well-being.

Balance: Balance underscores the importance of equilibrium in all aspects of life, avoiding extremes and fostering moderation. It involves harmonizing opposing forces and maintaining a sense of inner and outer balance.

Righteousness: Righteousness involves living in alignment with moral and ethical principles. It encompasses doing what is right, just, and ethical in all situations, contributing to the overall order and harmony of existence.

These principles collectively guide you on a path of virtuous living, contributing not only to personal well-being but also to the broader harmony of the community and the cosmos.

Embracing Ma'at involves a continuous journey of self-discovery, growth, and a commitment to living in accordance with these timeless principles.

Balance in Daily Life

How do you currently strive for balance and harmony in your daily life?

....

....

....

....

....

....

In what areas of your life do you feel a need for greater balance, and how might you achieve it?

....

....

....

....

....

Truth & Integrity

Reflect on a recent situation where you upheld truth and integrity. How did it feel?

....

....

....

....

....

Are there instances where you could have been more truthful or acted with greater integrity? How might you approach such situations in the future?

....

....

....

....

....

Justice & Fairness

How do you contribute to justice and fairness in your community or social circles?

_____

_____

_____

_____

_____

_____

Are there biases or prejudices you need to confront within yourself to contribute to a more just and fair society?

_____

_____

_____

_____

_____

Reciprocity & Mutual Support

Reflect on the relationships in your life. How do you practice reciprocity and mutual support?

In what ways can you enhance the supportive nature of your relationships?

TAKE A BREAK

---

1. What is the origin of Kemetic spirituality?

    A) Greece   C) Rome

    B) Ancient Egypt   D) Mesopotamia

2. In Kemetic spirituality, what does Ma'at represent?

    A) Chaos & disorder   C) Love & beauty

    B) Underworld & death   D) Balance & harmony

3. Who is considered a primary god in Kemetic spirituality?

    A) Ra   C) Odin

    B) Zeus   D) Shiva

TAKE A BREAK

---

4. What does the term "Kemetic" derive from?

A) The Greek word for 'knowledge'

C) The ancient Egyptian name for Egypt – Kemet

B) An ancient African language meaning 'life'

D) The Latin word for 'spirit'

---

5. What is the central belief of Kemetic spirituality?

A) The belief in a single deity

C) The belief in reincarnation

B) The belief that there are no deities, only universal energy

D) The belief in multiple gods & goddesses, each with their own domain

Personal Growth & Transformation

In what ways are you currently pursuing personal growth and transformation?

....

....

....

....

....

....

How might aligning with the principles of Ma'at enhance your journey of self-discovery?

....

....

....

....

....

....

Community Engagement

How are you involved in your community, and in what ways can you contribute positively?

_____

_____

_____

_____

_____

_____

Reflect on the concept of unity and how you can foster a sense of community around you.

_____

_____

_____

_____

_____

Harmony with Nature

How do you connect with and honor the natural world in your daily life?

_____

_____

_____

_____

_____

_____

In what ways could you harmonize more with the natural world in your life?

_____

_____

_____

_____

_____

_____

SACRED CYCLES

These next few pages are for women who are still experiencing a menstrual cycle. For those women who have transitioned from this phase in life—congratulations—feel free to skip ahead to the next section. For those still in the midst of this experience, please continue reading.

The practice of observing the natural menstrual cycle aligns beautifully with the principles at the heart of Kemetic spirituality. In Kemetic spirituality, harmony with nature is paramount, and the menstrual cycle, influenced by lunar phases and cosmic cycles, reflects this interconnectedness.

The recognition of the sacred feminine energy within the menstrual cycle also resonates with Kemetic beliefs, where the divine feminine is revered as a potent force in the cosmic tapestry.

Moreover, the observation of the menstrual cycle resonates with Kemetic spirituality's focus on life's cyclical nature and perpetual cycles of renewal. This alignment with Ma'at—the cosmic balance and order—makes acknowledging the balance inherent in the female body's cyclical nature a tangible expression of the sacred and interconnected journey of life.

In essence, observing the natural menstrual cycle within the context of Kemetic spirituality becomes a sacred act, symbolizing the participation in the cosmic rhythms and the divine order woven into the fabric of existence.

Our menstrual cycles serve as a reminder that life is precious and inherently cyclical. Each phase of this cycle is not only necessary but also sacred. Contrary to what patriarchal societies often teach us, our lives aren't meant to be linear or constantly productive. There are ebbs and flows, periods of rest and renewal, and period of growth and expansion.

By embracing our sacred feminine flow and recognizing ourselves as part of this sacred cycle, we align more closely with the rhythms of life itself. In doing so, we honor not only ourselves, but also every life we touch, and the sustainability of our future.

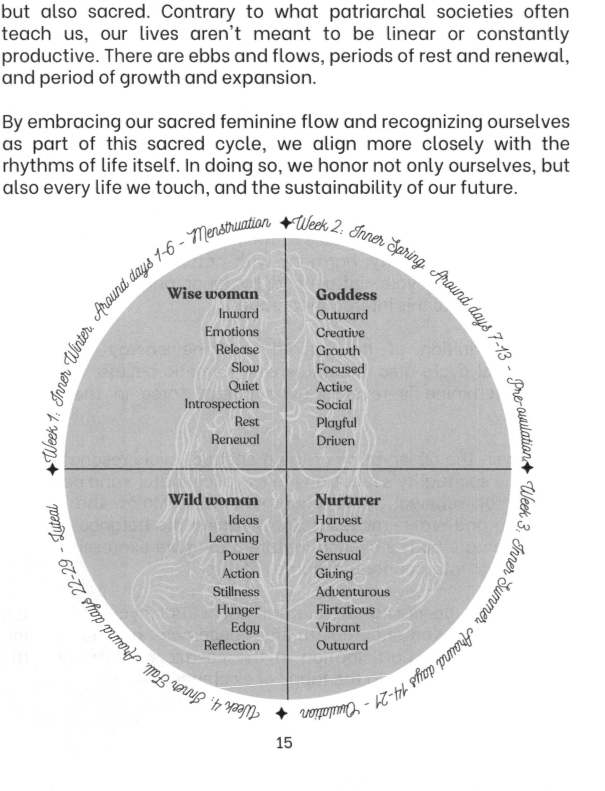

Week 1: Inner Winter. Around days 1-6 - Menstruation

Week 2: Inner Spring. Around days 7-13 - Pre-ovulation

Week 3: Inner Summer. Around days 14-21 - Ovulation

Week 4: Inner Fall. Around days 22-29 - Luteal

Wise woman
Inward
Emotions
Release
Slow
Quiet
Introspection
Rest
Renewal

Goddess
Outward
Creative
Growth
Focused
Active
Social
Playful
Driven

Wild woman
Ideas
Learning
Power
Action
Stillness
Hunger
Edgy
Reflection

Nurturer
Harvest
Produce
Sensual
Giving
Adventurous
Flirtatious
Vibrant
Outward

CYCLE TRACKING

To better attune yourself to your own sacred cycle, starting at the beginning of your next cycle (the first day of your bleed), for that entire cycle, record any associated thoughts, feelings, or behaviors that accompany that phase of your cycle. I have added rough estimations of the potential phase below, however you may need to adjust this based on your own cycle.

If you're having trouble identifying your menstrual cycle phase, don't worry. There are many online resources available to assist you. For instance, signs like an "egg-white" like discharge or specific body temperature changes could show ovulation.

MENSTRUATION

PRE-OVULATION

OVULATION

LUTEAL

Reflect on the ways in which you acknowledge the cyclical nature of your body and the phases of your menstrual cycle.

Consider how you integrate self-care practices that align with each phase, embracing the unique energy and needs that arise during menstruation, pre-ovulation, ovulation, and the pre-menstrual phase.

Explore the connection between your internal rhythms and how you show up in the external world—in your relationships, career, and personal self-expression.

If your cycle is irregular, consider exploring natural remedies to restore its regularity. For instance, acupuncture and naturopathy are powerful modalities in the world of natural healing.

Reflections:

Living a Ma'at-Centric Life

Envision your life when living in alignment with the principles of Ma'at. What changes can you make to move closer to this vision?

_____

_____

_____

_____

_____

_____

How can you infuse Ma'at into your thoughts, actions, and intentions on a daily basis?

_____

_____

_____

_____

_____

Facing Challenges

Consider a recent challenge. How might applying the principles of Ma'at guide your response and resolution?

_____

_____

_____

_____

_____

Are there aspects of your approach to challenges that are incongruent with Ma'at? How can you realign?

_____

_____

_____

_____

_____

Continuous Reflection

Commit to regular reflection of these principles. How will you incorporate Ma'at reflection into your daily, weekly, or monthly routine? *e.g. Perhaps you will commit to checking in with the principles at the beginning or end of each month to remind yourself of them and how you are applying them in your life.*

....

....

....

....

....

....

....

....

....

....

ALIGNING WITH YOUR SOUL

Central to Kemetic spirituality is the importance of forming a deep connection with your own soul, or Ka as it's known. This process paves the way for inner wisdom, spiritual growth, and alignment with Ma'at—the cosmic order. Regarded as a divine spark within each person, the Ka embodies our eternal and immortal aspects.

To connect with this divine essence requires an introspective journey. It means delving into deeper levels of consciousness to unlock innate wisdom and purpose that lie within you.

Ultimately in Kemetic spirituality, recognizing that every person carries within them a divine spark—a reservoir of wisdom—holds immense significance. Accessing this wellspring propels you towards an enlightened existence filled with purpose.

THE KA AND BA

In ancient Egyptian cosmology, human beings were believed to be composed of multiple parts. Among these, two significant aspects were the Ka and the Ba. The concepts of Ka and Ba play pivotal roles in guiding you on your journey towards spiritual evolution.

⊔ Ka: The Body of the Soul

The Ka represents your unique spiritual counterpart. It is the light body that exists through 3D-6D and allows you to anchor in your soul and higher-self across these dimensions into this realm. It is literally a vehicle for the higher-self to descend into matter. Every person has one, however, most people, unless they have consciously activated and worked with it, have a dormant one.

🦅 Ba: The Higher Self

The Ba symbolizes the transcendent, spiritual aspect, associated with wisdom, guidance, and a deeper understanding of your life path. Unlike the Ka, which might be seen as a spiritual companion closely linked to personal experiences, the Ba is often viewed as a more universal and enlightened aspect of you. It reflects a broader, more transcendent connotation, often associated with higher wisdom and a connection to universal truths.

These concepts offer profound insights into the multi-dimensional nature of Kemetic spirituality, where the Ka embodies a personal and experiential connection, and the Ba represents a transcendent and universal aspect of the self. Together, they contribute to a comprehensive understanding of spiritual identity and continuity in the intricate tapestry of existence.

HIGHER-SELF MEDITATION

Begin by finding a quiet and comfortable space where you won't be disturbed. Sit down with your spine straight and close your eyes.

Take a few deep breaths, inhaling through your nose and exhaling through your mouth, letting go of any tension with each breath.

Visualize roots extending from the base of your spine, reaching deep into the Earth, anchoring you securely. Feel the supportive energy of the Earth flowing up through these roots, grounding and stabilizing you.

As you deepen your connection with the Earth, shift your focus upward, directing your attention to the crown of your head. Imagine a string lighting up from your crown chakra.

Follow this string for about 1 foot (12 inches), here you will find your soul star chakra. It may be easier to visualize this as a bright white or yellow light.

Feel a sense of calm and clarity as you connect with your higher-self, gaining insights and guidance that will support you on your journey.

Take your time in this space of connection, and when you're ready, gently return to the present moment, carrying the serenity of this experience with you.

Do this practice regularly to deepen your connection.

Soul Calling

Consider the questions, "Who am I?", "Why am I here?" Consider the roles you play in your life, the labels you identify with, and the qualities that define your true self.

Reflect on your unique gifts, talents, and passions. How do these aspects contribute to your sense of self, and how can you nurture them further?

....

....

....

....

....

....

Identify activities or experiences that consistently bring you joy. What is it about these moments that resonate with your true self?

....

....

....

....

....

....

Consider whether there are aspects of your life where joy is lacking. How can you incorporate more of what brings you joy into your daily routine?

....

....

....

....

....

....

Reflect on moments in your life when you felt a deep sense of fulfillment or purpose. What activities, skills, or energies were you engaged in during those moments?

....

....

....

....

....

....

What do you believe you are here to gift humanity with? Is it your artistic expression, the healing power of your voice, your loving presence, or a combination of these and more?

_____

_____

_____

_____

_____

How can you intentionally share and offer your gifts to positively impact those around you?

_____

_____

_____

_____

_____

WOMB CHANTING

Womb chanting, often associated with sacred feminine energy, is believed to have positive effects on creativity and expression of your soul. This practice involves directing vocal vibrations towards the womb with the goal of activating and boosting energy flow in this powerful center.

While there isn't direct historical evidence specifically detailing womb chanting as a practice in ancient Egypt, Kemetic spirituality did emphasize the sacredness of the feminine, particularly through goddess worship and rituals related to fertility and creation.

Womb chanting is believed to spark creativity and inspiration by releasing emotional blockages stored in the pelvic region, paving the way for emotional freedom which can fuel creative pursuits.

Furthermore, womb chanting is linked with balancing and aligning the sacral chakra—our body's energy hub responsible for creativity, passion, and pleasure. Through this ritualistic practice, you may find a deeper connection with your feminine energy, fostering enhanced intuition, confidence, and empowerment.

Seen as a grounding ritual that provides stability for creative expression, womb chanting is often regarded as deeply transformative—a spiritually enriching practice that aligns you with the natural cycles of creation and renewal.

In essence, participating in womb chanting rituals offers an all-encompassing approach to connecting with your soul essence ; it merges physical sensations with emotional experiences and spiritual elements to amplify self-expression and personal growth.

LET'S CHANT

Find a quiet and comfortable space where you can sit or lie down.

Take a few deep breaths to center yourself. Feel your connection to the Earth beneath you, allowing any tension to release as you exhale.

Bring your awareness towards your womb space, located in the lower part of your abdomen, deep within your pelvic region.

Breathe deeply into this space, visualizing a warm, golden light filling this sacred space. Envision the energy flowing freely, connecting you to the creative and intuitive power within.

Begin to notice there is a sound in your womb that wants to be expressed vocally.

Start releasing this sound by humming, or making other gentle sounds. Trust the intuitive connection between your womb and throat, allowing the expression to unfold organically.

Be mindful that as you chant, deep emotions, particularly grief or pain, may surface. Acknowledge these emotions without judgment, understanding that this process is a transformative journey. Allow yourself to fully release any emotional energy that emerges.

As you continue with the chanting practice, observe how the process evolves.

Over time, you may notice a shift from pain to pleasure, or vice versa, in the vocalization. Embrace the pain and the pleasure that arises from the sounds, celebrating the healing and creative potential unlocked through this practice.

After the session, take a moment for reflection. Journal your experiences, noting any insights, emotions, or changes in perception. Integrate these reflections into your daily life, carrying the transformative energy of womb chanting with you.

Reflections:

....

....

....

....

....

....

....

....

Soul Expression

Where in your life do you sense you might be holding yourself back? Explore any fears, self-doubts, or limiting beliefs that might be contributing to this restraint.

Reflect on instances where you've bitten your tongue or held back your true thoughts and feelings. What emotions or concerns prompted you to do so?

Explore the impact of not expressing yourself fully. Are there recurring situations where open communication could lead to greater understanding or resolution?

Identify areas of your life where your voice deserves to be heard more clearly. This could be in relationships, work, or personal pursuits.

Consider the potential positive outcomes of speaking up and sharing your thoughts. How might your authentic voice contribute to personal growth and meaningful connections?

Reflect on your current state of self-expression. In what areas of your life do you feel you are not embodying the ultimate expression of yourself?

....

....

....

....

....

Explore the gap between your current state and your ideal self-expression. What changes or actions could bring you closer to being the fullest and most authentic version of yourself?

....

....

....

....

....

HONORING YOURSELF

In Kemetic spirituality, forming a bond with yourself is a journey that involves exploring and understanding your inner world. By nurturing this bond with yourself, you set off on a transformative path towards self-awareness, self-control, and alignment with Ma'at's principles—the cosmic order.

Practices in aiding this self-connection include introspection, mindfulness, and developing inner virtues. Through these deliberate actions, you aim to bring your thoughts, feelings, and actions into harmony. This promotes balance and aligns you with your higher purpose. Seeing the act of connecting with yourself as sacred helps you to live life authentically and honestly while deeply understanding your unique role in the larger cosmic order.

WHY HONOR SELF?

In a world where the complexity of modern life pulls us in a myriad of directions, finding moments to honor ourselves can feel like navigating through a bustling marketplace—overwhelming, chaotic, and often neglected. This chapter serves as a sanctuary amidst the chaos, a gentle reminder to pause, breathe, and reconnect with the sacred temple that is you.

In today's fast-paced world, the pursuit of self-love, self-compassion, and self-worth can often feel like faint echoes lost in the noisy chatter of social media, temptation towards substance abuse, and never-ending daily responsibilities. We live in an age where disconnection—from ourselves, from each other, and from the natural rhythms of life—has become all too common. The constant buzz of notifications, the ever-scrolling feed, the numbing allure of drugs, alcohol, and food—these modern distractions threaten to drown out the whispers of our souls, leaving us adrift in a sea of superficiality.

However, in these challenging times, the ancient wisdom of Kemetic spirituality provides guidance—it serves as a beacon of hope amidst darkness. It teaches us that true fulfillment isn't found in materialistic pleasures but in deep connection with ourselves and the divine essence present throughout creation.

And here exists its sacred invitation—to reclaim our sovereignty, to honor the divine vessel that houses our essence, and to tend to the multifaceted layers of our being. This section beckons you to journey inward, to explore the depths of your being with curiosity and compassion, and to cultivate a sense of reverence for the miracle that is you.

In a world that constantly tries to divide us, Kemetic spirituality offers unity—a path back to ourselves and back to our divine origins. It reminds us that even amidst modern chaos, the most precious treasure lies within each one of us—waiting to be uncovered, and waiting to be embraced.

As we delve into this exploration of self-love, self-compassion, and holistic well-being, I invite you to navigate with tenderness and grace, honoring the wisdom of your body, mind, and spirit. May this chapter serve as a guiding light, illuminating the path towards greater self-awareness, resilience, and an unwavering commitment to nurture the temple of your soul amidst the clamor of the modern world.

TAKE A BREAK

FIND YOUR WAY BACK HOME TO SELF

Self-Love

Reflect on areas in your life where you struggle to love yourself unconditionally. What specific thoughts or beliefs contribute to a lack of self-love in these areas?

Consider how childhood wounds or experiences with your immediate family might have influenced your self-perception. Are there patterns that you can identify and work towards healing?

Self-Worth

Investigate areas of your life where you do not feel worthy. What aspects of yourself or your experiences have led to feelings of unworthiness?

_____

_____

_____

_____

_____

_____

_____

_____

_____

_____

_____

Reflect on how these feelings of unworthiness may be impacting what you allow yourself to receive in life. Are there opportunities or experiences you subconsciously block due to feelings of inadequacy?

Self-Compassion

List three qualities you appreciate about yourself.

....

....

....

List 3 perceived 'flaws', or things that you find difficult to appreciate in yourself. How can you cultivate a deeper sense of self-love by embracing your imperfections?

....

....

....

....

....

....

....

....

Consider how extending unconditional love to yourself can positively impact your overall well-being and relationships

SELF-LOVE PRACTICE

Download the free Heart Healing meditation

1. Notice what you say to yourself, consciously or subconsciously.

One way to become aware of your negative self talk is by noticing when you feel bad, and then by thinking what was the thought that you had just before that bad feeling?

Practice cancelling and clearing the negative thought and replacing it with a positive affirmation. For example, replace "You're so stupid, you can't do anything right", with "I am intelligent and I can do this."

2. Notice that part of you that notices that you struggle (the compassionate witness).

As the compassionate witness, love that part of you that is active in the struggle. Meet it with love, patience and understanding.

3. Put your hand on your heart and talk to this part of you as if you were a parent or a friend or a lover. Tell it you love it.

Try to to do this whenever you feel a struggle.

4. Have gratitude and appreciation for who you are and what you're doing to heal.

5. Keep committing to yourself every day, keep your word.

6. Celebrate your achievements (don't skip this step!).

Physical Well-being

Reflect on your current practices for nurturing your body and overall health, such as through exercise, nutrition, rest, and mindfulness.

....

....

....

....

....

....

Are you prioritizing activities that contribute to your physical well-being? Identify any areas where you can enhance your physical self-care routine.

....

....

....

....

....

....

Emotional Well-being

Reflect on how you currently manage and take care of your emotions. Are you giving yourself the necessary time and space to process your feelings?

....

....

....

....

....

Consider whether you respect and acknowledge your emotions without judgment. Are there areas where you can create more space for your emotions to arise naturally?

....

....

....

....

....

Mental Well-being

Explore your strategies for managing and caring for your mindset, programming, and beliefs. Are you conscious of the thoughts that shape your mental landscape?

....

....

....

....

....

Where have you noticed you have unintentionally created negative realities due to your own thoughts? What about positive realities due to positive thoughts?

....

....

....

....

....

Consider whether your mental habits contribute positively to your well-being. Are there any limiting beliefs or negative thought patterns that you can address and transform?

LIMITING BELIEF / NEGATIVE THOUGHT PATTERN	EMPOWERING BELIEF / POSITIVE THOUGHT PATTERN

Etheric Body

Reflect on your practices for managing and looking after your etheric body. Are you engaged in energy work, such as caring for your meridians and chakras? This could include practices such as Reiki, Sound healing, Bodywork, EFT, and Acupuncture.

....

....

....

....

....

What grounding routines do you incorporate into your daily life to nurture and balance your etheric body? This could include practices such as walking barefoot in nature, or engaging in mindfulness exercises that anchor you in the present moment.

....

....

....

....

....

EFT

Emotional Freedom Technique (EFT), also known as tapping, is a powerful method that combines elements of ancient Chinese acupressure with modern psychology to address and transform negative beliefs while balancing the body's energy meridians.

By gently tapping on specific meridian points on the body, such as those used in traditional acupuncture, EFT aims to release emotional blockages and restore the flow of energy. This process is particularly effective in addressing negative beliefs that may be limiting your potential or hindering personal growth.

EFT is not only a technique for immediate relief but also a transformative tool for long-term change. When you tap on specific acupressure points while verbalizing negative beliefs or emotions, you engage in a dual process that combines physical touch with focused mental attention.

This dual-action approach helps to rewire the brain, creating new neural pathways and disrupting the ingrained patterns associated with negative beliefs.

As a result, you may experience a shift in your emotional state and a newfound sense of balance. Regular practice of EFT can lead to a profound transformation by allowing you to let go of deeply rooted negative beliefs, fostering emotional resilience, and promoting overall well-being.

EFT, through its focus on energy meridians and emotional healing, aligns with Kemetic spirituality by addressing the interconnectedness of mind, body, and spirit in the pursuit of holistic well-being.

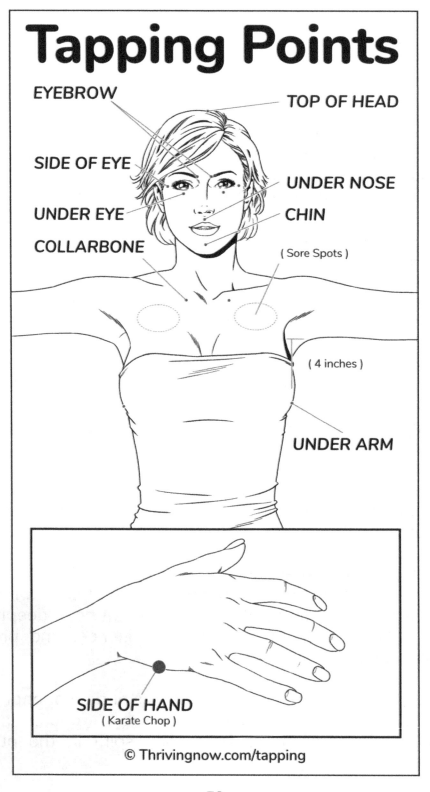

Tapping Points

EYEBROW

TOP OF HEAD

SIDE OF EYE

UNDER NOSE

UNDER EYE

CHIN

COLLARBONE

(Sore Spots)

(4 inches)

UNDER ARM

SIDE OF HAND
(Karate Chop)

© Thrivingnow.com/tapping

LET'S TAP

Take one limiting belief you wrote down previously, and follow the process below:

Tap with two fingers using a gentle yet firm pressure (not enough to hurt but enough to feel the tapping).

Setup:
Start tapping on the Karate Chop Point and repeat this setup phrase three times:

"Even though I feel (state your limiting belief, e.g., "like I can't make money from my soul work"), I deeply and completely love and accept myself."

Sequence:
Now, tap through the following points while repeating a reminder phrase at each one:

Eyebrow: "I feel (state your concern)."

Side of Eye: "This feeling (about your limiting belief)."

Under Eye: "It makes me feel (state your emotions)."

Under Nose: "I accept how I feel."

Chin: "Even if (your limiting belief), I'm open to acceptance."

Collarbone: "These feelings (about your limiting belief)."

Under Arm: "I choose to release and let go."

Top of Head: Repeat set up phrase: "Even though I feel (state your your limiting belief, e.g., "like I can't make money from my soul work"), I deeply and completely love and accept myself."

Complete the Sequence steps until you begin to feel a sense of calm and relief about this belief, usually around 3–5 rounds.

5-4-3-2-1 METHOD

The 5-4-3-2-1 mindfulness exercise is a powerful grounding technique that aligns well with Kemetic spirituality to balance the etheric body.

Begin by acknowledging **five things you can see**, bringing your attention to the present moment. Connect this awareness to the visual symbols and elements around you, aligning with the principles of Ma'at.

Next, focus on **four things you can touch**, fostering a connection with the physical realm. This tactile engagement echoes the emphasis on the material world within Kemetic practices. It encourages a mindful presence in the body, promoting a harmonious balance.

Continue by recognizing **three things you can hear**, inviting the auditory senses to participate. In Kemetic spirituality, sound is often associated with rituals and prayers, linking you to the vibrational energy of the divine. This step reinforces the importance of resonance in maintaining etheric equilibrium.

Then, acknowledge **two things you can smell**, tapping into the olfactory senses. Scent has significance in spiritual practices, representing purification and connection. This aligns with the Kemetic emphasis on ritualistic cleansing for spiritual alignment.

Finally, focus on **one thing you can taste**, engaging the gustatory senses. This step echoes the concept of offerings and rituals involving food and drink in Kemetic traditions. By incorporating taste into grounding, you connect the physical act with spiritual significance, fostering a holistic approach to etheric balance.

FINDING INNER UNION

In Kemetic spirituality, the integration of masculine and feminine energies, holds particular significance, echoing the ancient Egyptian understanding of the interplay between opposites and the quest for balance. The ankh, a prominent symbol in Kemetic spirituality, encapsulates this duality, with its loop symbolizing the feminine and the staff representing the masculine, united in harmonious balance.

This spiritual tradition, deeply rooted in the worship of various deities embodying both masculine and feminine attributes, recognizes the inherent duality within the cosmos. The integration of masculine and feminine energies extends beyond external deities to the recognition of these energies within you also.

The union of masculine and feminine energies symbolizes the divine interconnection and harmonious balance necessary for cosmic order, reflecting the concept of Ma'at.

MASCULINE & FEMININE ENERGIES

Masculine and feminine energies, which transcend gender limitations, are universal principles that shape the essence of individuals and the dynamics of existence. Each person has both energies within themselves, creating a unique interplay that can, at times, be imbalanced. In our contemporary age, the pressures of a society often labeled as a "man's world" can lead many women to experience an overemphasis on masculinized energy, upsetting the equilibrium within.

An imbalance can lead to disharmony that can have an impact on many areas of your life—relationships, career, health—making the achievement of balance, or "inner union", not just necessary, but fundamental for personal harmony and spiritual health. Pursuing equilibrium allows you to harness the strength of both energies, promoting holistic personal growth and fulfillment.

The list below offers an example of the different energies, but is by no means exhaustive.

MASCULINE		FEMININE	
Logic	Linear	Intuition	Circular
Achieving	Constant	Experiencing	Changing
Doing	Logic	Being	Vision
Competition	Structure	Collaboration	Flow
Giving	Orienting	Receiving	Nurturing
Rational	Pursuing	Emotional	Deepening
Firm	External	Gentle	Internal
Mind	Strength	Heart	Compassion
Purpose	Focus	Pleasure	Adaptable
Deciding	Assertive	Feeling	Allowing

SIGNS OF IMBALANCE

Imbalances in masculine and feminine energies can manifest in various aspects of a person's life, impacting mental, emotional, and physical well-being. Often referred to as the 'wounded' aspects of these energies, signs of imbalance may include:

WOUNDED MASCULINE

Excessive Control: Struggling with a need to control situations and outcomes, often leading to rigidity and inflexibility.

Aggression: Expressing heightened aggression, impatience, or irritability in interactions with others.

Overemphasis on Logic: Relying excessively on logical thinking while neglecting intuitive or emotional aspects.

Workaholism: An obsessive focus on work and achievement, sometimes at the expense of personal relationships or self-care.

Emotional Detachment: Difficulty connecting with and expressing emotions, leading to emotional distance in relationships.

WOUNDED FEMININE

Over-Emotional Responses: Experiencing heightened emotional reactions or mood swings, potentially leading to instability.

Over-Nurturing: Overextending yourself to meet the needs of others, neglecting personal boundaries and self-care.

Indecision: Struggling with decision-making and feeling overwhelmed by choices.

Dependency: Excessive reliance on others for validation or a fear of being alone.

Lack of Assertiveness: Difficulty asserting yourself, setting boundaries, or expressing personal needs and desires.

Reflect on the balance between your masculine and feminine energies. How do these energies manifest in your daily life, and in what areas do you sense harmony or imbalance between them?

Explore the masculine traits within yourself. Are there aspects of assertiveness, logic, or ambition that dominate your approach to life? How might an overemphasis on these traits create imbalances in your overall energy?

Reflect on the presence of feminine qualities within you. How can a deeper embrace of your feminine traits contribute to a more balanced energy expression?

....

....

....

....

....

....

Examine situations where an imbalance in masculine energy may have influenced your actions. How did this imbalance impact your experiences and relationships?

....

....

....

....

....

Reflect on any wounds related to the feminine energy. Are there past experiences or societal influences that have shaped your perception of feminine traits?

....

....

....

....

....

....

How can acknowledging and healing these wounds contribute to a more balanced feminine expression?

....

....

....

....

....

....

SACRED SYMBOLISM

Throughout diverse spiritual traditions worldwide, the harmonious interplay between the masculine and feminine has been a recurring theme. Two prominent symbols embodying this balance are the Ankh, originating from ancient Egypt, and the Yin and Yang, rooted in Chinese philosophy.

In all aspects of life—be it love, career, or general existence—the Yin and Yang necessitate a delicate equilibrium of opposing forces to achieve harmony, symbolizing completion and the indispensable role of duality in maintaining balance. Rooted in Chinese philosophy, the Yin and Yang concept vividly illustrates the harmonious interdependence of opposing cosmic forces.

The Ankh, deeply ingrained in ancient Egyptian culture, holds profound significance across various life facets, embodying the essence of life. Its loop symbolizes the eternal and interconnected nature of existence, while the straight line signifies the linear and grounded aspects of life. In essence, the Ankh signifies the unity of opposites, proposing that embracing both cyclical and linear aspects is crucial for equilibrium.

Derived from Kemetic spirituality, the Ankh seamlessly aligns with the concept of Ma'at, underlining the interconnectedness and balance of cosmic forces. Despite its distinct Egyptian origin, the Ankh echoes a universal message similar to the Yin and Yang, emphasizing the need to embrace dualities for a harmonious and balanced life.

Yin · Dark · Moon · Water · Cold · Feminine · Softness · Passivenes

Yang · Light · Sun · Fire · Warm · Masculine · Hardness · Activeness

Masculine · Linear · Stability · Groundedness · Continuity · Penetrative

Feminine · Circular · Creation · Rebirth · Transformation · Receptive

Contemplate the concept of Yin and Yang, representing the feminine and masculine energies. How can you cultivate a harmonious interplay between these energies within your life, recognizing the cyclical and complementary nature of their dance?

TAKE A BREAK

---

1. What is a characteristic of masculine energy?

A) Nurturing

B) Intuitive

C) Protective

D) Emotional

---

2. Which of the following best describes feminine energy?

A) Dominant & controlling

B) Creative & nurturing

C) Passive & weak

D) Aggressive & assertive

---

3. What can be a result of imbalance between masculine and feminine energies within a person?

A) Stress, confusion, dissatisfaction

B) Increased physical strength

C) Enhanced creativity

D) Improved communication skills

TAKE A BREAK

---

4. Which statement about masculine and feminine energies is true?

A) Masculine energy is superior to feminine energy

B) Feminine energy is superior to masculine energy

C) Neither type of energy is superior; they are complementary

D) None of the above

5. How has society generally viewed masculine and feminine energies?

A) They are seen as equal in all aspects

B) Masculine energy is often valued more than feminine energy

C) Feminine energy is often valued more than masculine energy

D) Society does not differentiate between them

RELATING WITH OTHERS

Human connection holds a significant place in our lives, impacting our overall sense of well-being and belonging. The relationships we build provide emotional support, shared experiences, and help us form meaningful communities that foster personal growth and empathy. The quality of these bonds directly links to our self-worth. High self-worth lays the groundwork for genuine connections while unresolved internal issues can create tension in relationships.

In Kemetic spirituality, connecting with others carries deep importance as it aligns with Ma'at—representing harmony, balance, and interconnectedness. By nurturing positive relationships and aligning ourselves with Ma'at's principles, we not only enrich our spiritual journey but also add to collective wellness – highlighting life's interconnected nature as per Kemetic philosophy. Therefore, within this spiritual context, forging meaningful connections isn't just a personal goal but a sacred duty intertwined with Ma'at's universal order.

Relationships

Delve into past relationships where you may not have expressed love or received it fully. What patterns or behaviors emerged that reflected a lack of self-love or love for others?

Explore the impact of any abandonment, rejection or betrayal wounds you may carry from past relationships, including familial. How have these influenced your ability to give and receive love?

Consider your relationships with female friends. Are there any patterns or recurring themes in these connections that may indicate unresolved sisterhood wounds?

TAKE A BREAK

Find as many words as you can, there are 10 in total.
Words can go in any direction.
Words can share letters as they cross over each other.

```
C W W G K H A D O R A T I O N
W H A R M O N Y R S Z W Y U T
F R F D B C O N N E C T I O N
U C X A Q V T J X T N Z C J E
T U J P B H I I P T H G Q N M
O R U B J D F N I P T J D M T
F H J F S Q K N T R K L Y M I
F G W O U C W Z A I T H M D M
T C E P S E R V K T M N R L M
N O I T C E F F A R T A F M O
I N R F J S Y K B U T C C T C
P R P A R T N E R S H I P Y D
J R I H K O N O I T O V E D K
L Y H S N U U E G J S C B Y I
O V W A R K A J E N K B M C I
```

Answers:

```
C W W G K H A D O R A T I O N
W H A R M O N Y R S Z W Y U T
F R F D B C O N N E C T I O N
U C X A Q V T J X T N Z C J E
T U J P B H I I P T H G Q N M
O R U B J D F N I P T J D M T
F H J F S Q K N T R K L Y M I
F G W O U C W Z A I T H M D M
T C E P S E R V K T M N R L M
N O I T C E F F A R T A F M O
I N R F J S Y K B U T C C T C
P R P A R T N E R S H I P Y D
J R I H K O N O I T O V E D K
L Y H S N U U E G J S C B Y I
O V W A R K A J E N K B M C I
```

Word Bank

1. devotion
2. respect
3. trust
4. adoration
5. intimacy
6. partnership
7. harmony
8. affection
9. connection
10. commitment

66

Reflect on your relationship with your mother or maternal figures. What are the positive aspects that contribute to a healthy connection, and are there any areas of tension or unmet needs?

Reflect on your relationship with your father or paternal figures. What aspects of this connection bring you joy, and are there any unresolved conflicts or wounds?

Forgiveness

Explore instances where you may not have forgiven yourself. What actions or decisions from your past are challenging to forgive? How might releasing this burden contribute to your healing?

_____

_____

_____

_____

_____

_____

_____

_____

_____

_____

Reflect on situations where forgiveness towards others is needed. What resentments or unresolved emotions are hindering your ability to love freely? Can you commit to forgiving to the best of your ability?

HO'OPONOPONO

Ho'oponopono, an ancient Hawaiian ritual for forgiveness and healing, provides a pathway to let go of toxic energies within yourself. Obviously, this isn't a traditional Kemetic practice, however Ho'oponopono, with its emphasis on reconciliation, forgiveness, and healing, resonates with the Kemetic principles of balance, harmony, and the restoration of Ma'at. This process paves the way for transcendence into a higher, more divine state of being. In essence, Ho'oponopono translates to "making right twice".

At its core, it's about absolute freedom. Through forgiveness and acceptance of myself, I am able to extend the same grace towards you. Similarly, by forgiving and accepting you, I am essentially forgiving and accepting myself as well.

It can be practiced with 4 easy steps:

Step 1: Repentance – SAY: "I'M SORRY"

The first step is to take responsibility for the part you played in the relationship/the past/the situation. You acknowledge and accept what happened. You're sorry for holding onto all the anger, resentment, and shame for so long.

Step 2: Ask for Forgiveness – SAY: "PLEASE FORGIVE ME"

You ask another for forgiveness in the same way that you have forgiven them. Since you are one, you are both to be forgiven. You accept what has happened and accept it cannot be changed. You are saying please forgive me for holding onto this for far too long, please forgive me for the part I played in this situation.

Step 3: Gratitude – SAY: "THANK YOU"

It doesn't really matter who or what you're thanking. Thank your body for all it does for you. Thank yourself for being the best you can be. Thank yourself for the healing and the clearing. Be grateful for the experience, the lessons learned, and the opportunity to start anew. Thank God. Thank the Universe. Thank whoever it was that just forgave you. Just keep saying THANK YOU.

Step 4: Love – SAY: "I LOVE YOU"

Love heals all; it's the most potent force in the universe. When you extend love to another person, you're also showering love upon yourself, and vice versa. Express your love freely—towards the other, towards God, towards the Universe. Say I LOVE YOU to the air you breathe in, to the home that provides shelter for you. Embrace your challenges by saying I LOVE YOU. Repeat it constantly and sincerely mean it each time. Love alone has the power to heal; nothing rivals its strength

Do a separate Ho'oponopono process to forgive yourself and to forgive any others that you identified in the previous pages.

CONNECTING WITH THE DIVINE

Exploring spirituality often means seeking a deep connection with something greater than yourself—a divine presence that offers deeper understanding and alignment with the universal principles that govern life. This belief is found not just in Kemetic spirituality, but in many other traditions too; it suggests that this divine influence threads itself through all aspects of life, turning your journey towards self-discovery and spiritual growth into a sacred adventure in harmony with the cosmic order.

Intentional practices like meditation, surrender, and showing devotion can provide ways to communicate and work in harmony with this divine force. They allow us to tap into different aspects of creation. Such conscious connections don't just foster self-awareness and inner peace; they also help align our personal goals with larger divine plans. Regardless of which spiritual path we choose, this journey towards connecting with the divine ultimately leads us to recognize our own inherent divinity and encourages us to incorporate universal principles into every part of our lives.

BREATHWORK

The 7-11 breathing technique, involving inhaling for a count of seven and exhaling for a count of eleven, can facilitate a deeper connection with the divine in Kemetic spirituality. This rhythmic breathing pattern slows the breath and activates the parasympathetic nervous system, inducing a state of calmness and receptivity. As you enter this relaxed state, you create an internal environment conducive to spiritual attunement, enhancing your ability to connect with the divine forces.

───────────◆───────────

Find a quiet place where you can sit or lie down. Close your eyes and simply breathe in through your nose for a count of 7, focussing on pulling the breath all the way down into your diaphragm (you should feel your belly expand as you do so), then breathe out (through your nose or mouth) for a count of 11 (you should feel your belly contract as the air leaves your body).

Repeat this exercise for at least 5 breaths, but continue for longer if you can.

As you inhale and exhale, pay attention to the sensations in your body. Notice how each breath moves in and out, observe the rise and fall of your belly, feel any tingling sensation in your arms or legs, and recognize any tension or relaxation in your neck, back, or shoulders.

Once you feel fully relaxed, allow yourself to cultivate an awareness of a quiet still presence residing within and around you. This presence may carry with it an energy that feels like inner wisdom—an all-knowing intuition. It could also manifest as a profound connection with everything around you. You might also experience gentle waves of physical energy flowing throughout your body.

Unity Consciousness

Reflect on moments when you've felt a profound connection to everything around you. How does recognizing your oneness with the world impact your perspective and actions?

....

....

....

....

....

Explore instances where external events seemed to mirror your internal thoughts or emotions. What lessons or insights can be gained from viewing life as a series of reflections and reactions?

....

....

....

....

I Am Presence Awareness

Delve into moments when you felt a strong connection to a higher power within yourself. How does this awareness influence your daily life and decision-making?

....

....

....

....

....

Explore the concept of being Source energy incarnated. In what ways can you embody this realization more fully in your interactions with others and the world?

....

....

....

....

....

Higher-Self Anchoring

Reflect on experiences where you felt anchored into your higher-self. How did this anchoring influence your sense of self and decision-making?

Explore ways to enhance your connection with your higher-self. How can you invite the higher self more fully into your physical experience?

TAKE A BREAK

Unscramble the words below:

RDRESNURE   _____

UTNIY   _____

DIENVI   _____

NPCERSEE   _____

NARYOMH   _____

NSESENO   _____

ENCCNNOTOI   _____

EASCNTRNDECNE   _____

TNLMGNEHEITNE   _____

NODTIVOE   _____

Divine Surrender

Contemplate the idea of releasing the need for control and surrendering your lower mind (ego) to the wisdom of the higher mind (soul). What aspects of your life can benefit from letting go of control, allowing the flow of divine guidance to unfold?

....

....

....

....

Examine the lower mind goals or beliefs that may be holding you back from soul-aligned aspirations. What specific goals or patterns are you ready to release to create space for higher, more spiritually attuned goals?

....

....

....

....

Reflect on your relationship with surrender. How can you cultivate a sense of ease by surrendering to the natural flow of life and the divine? Consider instances where surrendering has led to positive outcomes.

_____

_____

_____

_____

_____

_____

Explore the concept of trusting in higher guidance. Are there areas of your life where you struggle to trust the unfolding journey? How can embracing trust enhance your surrender to the divine plan?

_____

_____

_____

_____

_____

_____

Contemplate the ease and joy that can accompany the act of releasing control. How can you approach surrendering with a light heart and a sense of freedom, knowing that it aligns you with the greater flow of existence?

....

....

....

....

....

....

Reflect on how surrendering to the flow of life helps you navigate uncertainty. How can surrender be a source of strength and resilience during times of change or unpredictability?

....

....

....

....

....

....

Consider the concept of divine timing and surrendering to the inherent wisdom of the universe. How can acknowledging and embracing divine timing ease any impatience or resistance you may feel towards the unfolding of your life's path?

....

....

....

....

....

....

Contemplate the role of acceptance in the surrender process. How can acceptance of the present moment and its unfolding events contribute to a more harmonious surrender to the flow of life?

....

....

....

....

....

....

GRATITUDE

Gratitude aligns with Kemetic spirituality by fostering a deep appreciation for the interconnectedness of all life and acknowledging the divine order, promoting harmony and balance in accordance with the principles of Ma'at.

It acts as a powerful bridge, connecting us to something greater than ourselves and helping us appreciate the abundance and beauty in our lives. When we nurture a heart full of gratitude, it changes how we see everyday moments, revealing the divine presence within them.

Expressing gratitude becomes more than just saying 'thank you'; it evolves into a sacred practice, an intimate conversation with that which bestows blessings upon us. This conscious recognition of life's positives opens up a pathway for divine energy to enter our awareness, aligning us harmoniously with the cosmic order around us.

Gratitude doesn't just strengthen our bond with the divine—it also transforms our consciousness, instilling within us humility and awe for the intricate tapestry of existence.

On the following page write a gratitude 'rant'. Allow your words to flow freely as you describe every aspect of your life that fills your heart with gratitude. This isn't just a list; it's an outpouring of heartfelt appreciation, a celebration of the countless blessings enriching your existence.

Gratitude rant

Devotion

Examine your devotion to yourself, your path, and your spiritual growth. In what ways does devotion inspire consistent action in your life?

Reflect on the balance between discipline and devotion. How can cultivating a loving devotion propel you forward on your spiritual path?

Hint: discipline is 'my feelings are irrelevant, I do what I need to do to get the results', while devotion asks us to tune in deeply and revel in the devotion that inspires us to take action.

CONNECTING WITH THE NETJERU

In the practice of Kemetic spirituality, forming a connection with the Netjeru—the divine deities of ancient Egypt—holds great significance. This bond creates a sacred bridge between humans and divinity, allowing us to tap into the profound wisdom and energy inherent in the ancient Egyptian pantheon. The Netjeru are revered as archetypal forces that embody cosmic order, providing you with access to a spiritual framework that aligns with Ma'at's principles - balance, truth, and cosmic harmony.

This relationship goes beyond mere religious practice; it is a transformative journey towards self-discovery and spiritual alignment. It provides guidance, strength, and inspiration in our personal lives. As mentors guiding our spiritual growth, the Netjeru become channels through which we can understand life's interconnectedness. They encourage us to embody their virtues while contributing to Ma'at's flourishing in both personal life and broader society.

Intention Setting

Clarify your intention for connecting with the Netjeru. What specific goals or transformations do you seek through this spiritual connection? Consider the broader impact on your personal growth and well-being.

Relationship with the Netjeru

Reflect on your current perception of the Netjeru and your relationship
with them. How do you see this relationship evolving, and what
feelings or beliefs shape your connection with these divine beings?

TAKE A BREAK

Match the deity to their characteristics:

Ra
Goddess of love, music, dance, fertility, and joy; often depicted as a cow or a woman with cow's horns.

Isis
Goddess of motherhood, magic, and fertility; symbol of divine femininity and nurturing.

Osiris
Sun god, creator, and bringer of light; symbolizes power and vitality.

Hathor
God of wisdom, writing, and knowledge; associated with the moon and magic.

Anubis
Lioness-headed goddess of war, healing, and protection.

Bastet
Goddess of home, fertility, and protection; often depicted as a lioness or a cat.

Thoth
God of the sky, kingship, and protection, Often depicted with the head of a falcon.

Ma'at
God of mummification, death, and the afterlife; guides souls in the underworld.

Sekhmet
Goddess of truth, justice, and cosmic balance; symbolizes order and harmony.

Horus
God of the afterlife, death, and resurrection; symbolizes rebirth and eternal life.

Answers:

Ra	Sun god, creator, and bringer of light; symbolizes power and vitality.
Isis	Goddess of motherhood, magic, and fertility; symbol of divine femininity and nurturing.
Osiris	God of the afterlife, death, and resurrection; symbolizes rebirth and eternal life.
Hathor	Goddess of love, music, dance, fertility, and joy; often depicted as a cow or a woman with cow's horns.
Anubis	God of mummification, death, and the afterlife; guides souls in the underworld.
Bastet	Goddess of home, fertility, and protection; often depicted as a lioness or a cat.
Thoth	God of wisdom, writing, and knowledge; associated with the moon and magic.
Ma'at	Goddess of truth, justice, and cosmic balance; symbolizes order and harmony.
Sekhmet	Lioness-headed goddess of war, healing, and protection.
Horus	God of the sky, kingship, and protection; often depicted with the head of a falcon.

Deity Connection

Explore different Egyptian deities, and reflect on any intuitive connections you may feel. Have you already formed a bond with a specific deity? Pay attention to any that have called to you through signs, symbols, dreams or other means.

Identify the qualities or aspects of the deity you resonate with. What attributes of theirs do you wish to embody more in your life?

CREATE AN ALTAR

An altar serves as a sacred space where spiritual practices like rituals, prayers, and offerings can be made. While not every practitioner adopts this practice, having an altar can provide a centered space for your craft.

1. Begin by selecting a space, on a table, shelf, windowsill, or any flat surface.

2. Clear the chosen surface and clean it with an appropriate cleanser. Treat the altar as sacred; remove any non-sacred items cluttering the space.

3. Gather items representing each element, e.g. candle for fire, feather for air, cup/bowl for water, crystal/rock for earth.

4. Personalize your altar with items resonating with your spiritual practice. Arrange items intentionally, considering symbolism and energy.

5. Choose a cleansing method to cleanse the space the altar resides, e.g. salt cleanse, sound, or sage/palo santo. Ensure every corner, door, floor, and ceiling is cleansed.

6. Set an intention for your altar's purpose, either general or specific.

7. Communicate boundaries to those sharing your living space, ensuring respect for your sacred space.

What elements, symbols, and items would you like to add to your altar for your chosen deity. Consider what offerings you can present to your chosen deity as a gesture of reverence.

TAKE A BREAK

Use the blank page to draw your envisioned altar. Consider symbols such as the Ankh, a statue or image of the deity, the eye of Ra, as well as any color symbolism such as gold.

INVOCATION

An invocation is a sacred prayer calling upon the divine for presence, guidance, and blessings. It establishes a tangible connection with the spiritual realm, inviting specific deities to actively participate in your sacred space or life. Express your reverence and intentions during the invocation, seeking guidance, protection, and blessings from the invoked gods and goddesses.

1. Engage in a self-purification ritual or ritual bath before any significant spiritual tasks. Ritual baths can include herbs, essential oils, Epsom salts, or specific ingredients aligning with your intention. A shower would also be beneficial.

2. Cleanse the space before any significant spiritual tasks, e.g. using sound (drums, chimes, singing bowl), or sage/palo santo.

3. Visualize yourself surrounded by a golden bubble of light.

4. Practice a grounding and centering meditation to connect with the Earth's energies and focus your intent.

5. Set an intention for your practice.

6. If you desire, you may call in your own spiritual team to create a supportive and protected environment, this is up to personal beliefs and preferences.

7. Invoke the chosen deity, you may refer to the invocation on the following page as an example.

8. Spend some time connecting with the deity in this sacred space, paying attention to any feelings, sensations, thoughts or other communications that come forth.

9. Ensure you close the space:
- thank the deity (and your spiritual team)
- politely dismiss them
- visualize the closure of any energetic portals and the release of any remaining energy or connections back into the universe
- call all of your own energy back to you.

10. Verbally declare that the ritual or ceremony is now complete.

––––––––––––––◆––––––––––––––

One example of an invocation that you may use in your practice is as follows:

"Divine [God/Goddess Name of Deity or Divine Essence], I call upon your presence and grace.

In this sacred moment, I open my heart and mind to your divine energy.

May your wisdom and love flow through me, guiding my steps on this sacred path.

I seek your guidance, protection, and blessings, as I embark on this journey of [state the purpose or intention].

With reverence and humility, I welcome your presence, and I offer my sincere devotion and gratitude.

Thank you, thank you, thank you."

––––––––––––––◆––––––––––––––

Important points:

Maintain consistency with your practice, connecting regularly, like any relationship, this is one that develops over time.

Approach any spiritual practice, like an invocation, with profound respect; they are not matters to be taken lightly or 'messed around' with.

Initiate the practice of invocations to establish communion with your chosen deity. Reflect on the experience and note any insights or feelings that arise during these rituals.

DIVINATION

When practicing divination, it's important to understand that the power of any tool depends largely on your own intuitive abilities to interpret them. Therefore, in this section we will emphasize nurturing and refining your innate intuition, with the goal being to foster a deep understanding that wisdom comes from within you. This will simultaneously reduce your overreliance on external tools, while at the same time improve your use of external divination tools.

There are many ways to develop your intuition, here are a couple of practices to try:

Engage with Direct (Literal) Intuition

1. Find a quiet spot where you can sit comfortably.

2. Practice the 7-11 breath, counting to 7 on your inhale and 11 on your exhale. Repeat for 5 breaths.

3. Bring to mind an event or situation you'd like more insight about.

4. Dedicate a few minutes to deeply focus on this event or situation. Don't come to any conclusions, leave it open.

5. Invite a direct intuitive experience related to this event in the near future.

6. Release it from your thoughts, and trust that you'll receive some insight when the time is right.

Write below the event or situation you are looking for more insight on, along with any initial insights you have about it.

Come back later to record the insights you received, and how these insights came to you.

How did this align with your inital thoughts?

I am looking for insight on:

....

....

....

I received the following insights :

....

....

....

....

....

....

Work with indirect (symbolic) intuition:

1. Ask yourself "What does my life need right now?" Repeat this three times, taking a moment between each repetition. Imagine that each time you ask the question, you're moving closer to a more meaningful answer.

2. Once you've asked the question the third time, pick up your pen and sketch one symbol below.

3. Interpret this symbol. What does it suggest? Does it hint at something you should add or remove from your life? Or perhaps it signifies something you should do more of?

Ego vs Intuition

Take a moment to think back to a recent instance when you experienced panic, anxiety or some other uncertainty. Can you remember the fear-driven thoughts that surfaced at this time? Ponder on the emotions and tone associated with these thoughts. What did that 'inner voice' of the ego sound like? Was it speaking rapidly? Did the thoughts cascade one after another? What did you feel in your body? Write down any other details you can recollect.

Reflect on a recent situation where you felt an inner calmness, secure in the knowing that everything was fine. Can you remember the thoughts, or perhaps the lack of thought, that surfaced? How did the voice of your intuition sound? Was it quiet and reassuring? Was it slow and steady? What did you feel in your body? How different was it from the voice of the ego? Write down anything else you can recall from this experience.

ASK FOR A SIGN

Asking for a "sign" from the cosmos or divine entities is a common practice when seeking guidance. It involves understanding the universe's subtle language and being open to symbols with personal meaning. This act shows faith and connection, whether prompted by a question, uncertainty, or the need for validation. It bridges the gap between the seen and unseen realms.

Interpreting these signs requires personal intuition and context, allowing for spiritual dialogue and alignment with forces beyond our understanding. Signs can be anything, including seeing specific animals, number sequences, phrases, or having unexpected encounters.

Invite your chosen deity to provide you with a sign confirming their presence in your life.

My sign:

....

Reflections upon receiving it:

....

....

....

....

Dream Interpretation

Reflect on any memorable dreams that still reside in your memory. Research any animals, signs, or symbols present in these dreams and ponder upon your interpretation of them as they relate to your life. What messages do you believe these dreams were trying to convey?

PENDULUM DOWSING

Pendulum dowsing is a divination practice that involves the use of a pendulum—a weighted object suspended from a string or chain—to gain insights or answer questions. In this practice, we'll use the pendulum as a bridge to your own internal guidance and intuition.

As well as developing trust in your innate intuition, pendulum use can enhance your connection with deities by strengthening your ability to receive subtle spiritual insights and messages. As you become more attuned to the movements and responses of the pendulum, you develop a heightened sensitivity to the energies around you.

While it may be possible to use a pendulum to connect with deities directly, this should be left to those who are experienced and well-practiced in this art. It's important not to underestimate these tools; instead, we should treat them with due respect, recognizing their sacredness and power.

1. Before use, cleanse and charge your pendulum. This can be done through methods like placing it in the light of the full moon, using sage smoke, or burying it in salt.

2. In a quiet space, with a calm and clear mind, hold on to the top end of your pendulum's chain so it can swing freely.

3. First establish a baseline by asking the pendulum for your "Yes", "No," and "Maybe" signals.

Yes: ....

No: ....

Maybe: ....

4. Test these signals by asking straightforward questions that have known answers; ensure the answers align with your baseline yes, no, and maybe signals.

5. You're now ready to ask more complex questions; keep them clear and concise so it can be answered as a yes or no. If the pendulum answers maybe or remains still, it indicates that it either can't answer that question or it can't answer yet.

Ethical considerations to keep in mind:

- Avoid using your pendulum when emotionally or mentally unsteady as this could lead to inaccurate responses. Consider asking your pendulum before starting: "Is now a good time to dowse?"
- Use the pendulum for positive and constructive aims. Refrain from posing questions that might inflict harm, distress, or unnecessary anxiety.
- Maintain honesty with yourself and others. If there's uncertainty about interpretation, admit it openly rather than manipulating the pendulum's responses to suit a particular narrative.
- Don't substitute medical expertise with your pendulum use— never put yourself at risk—if faced with serious health concerns, always seek professional medical help.
- Avoid using the pendulum to delve into someone else's private life without their permission—respect their privacy rights.
- When intending to use the pendulum on behalf of someone else, always ask their permission first; they should understand they have every right to decline if they wish.
- Understand the limited nature of pendulums. At times, it may be more useful to consult other forms of divination that can provide more layered and comprehensive answers.
- Don't become dependent on pendulum dowsing. While it's a form of divination that can assist you in making decisions, it shouldn't serve as your only method for doing so.

HONORING THE ANCESTORS

In Kemetic spirituality, honoring your ancestors plays a pivotal role, emphasizing a deep connection between the living and their ancestors. This belief stems from the idea that our ancestors' spirits live on, actively influencing our lives by providing guidance, protection, and blessings. The act of ancestral veneration involves paying respect to your predecessors while acknowledging their ongoing impact on your life and recognizing their continued existence in the spiritual realm.

You can engage in rituals, offerings, and prayers to express gratitude, seek guidance, and establish a harmonious connection with your ancestors. This connection is not only a means of honoring lineage but also a way to tap into the wisdom and experiences of those who came before. Ancestral veneration in Kemetic spirituality aligns with the principles of Ma'at, fostering balance, order, and reciprocity between the realms of the living and the ancestral spirits.

FAMILY TREE

Create a detailed family tree, going back as far as you can go.

Research and document the experiences of your ancestors—what challenges they faced, triumphs they celebrated, and the environments they navigated.

Consider how their emotional landscape might have influenced your own. Did they carry the weight of unspoken traumas, resilience, or joy?

Explore mental patterns that may have been handed down through generations, whether it be approaches to problem-solving, coping mechanisms, or ways of thinking.

Assess if there are recurring themes related to money, such as abundance or scarcity mentalities, financial successes, or challenges. Recognizing these patterns allows you to gain insight into your own relationship with finances.

Explore the concept of ancestral shame. Write down any inherited feelings of guilt, shame, or unresolved emotions within your family history. Acknowledge these emotions and contemplate how they may be influencing your present mindset.

TAKE A BREAK

Play some Sudoku: Fill every empty cell in the grid with a number from 1 to 9. Each row, column, and 3 x 3 box within the grid must contain all numbers from 1 to 9 without repetition.

8				2		7		
	1	9			5	3		2
	5		6		7			
		1				9		5
	2						3	
9		3				8		
		9		6		1		
3		4	7			5	8	
		5		8				9

Reflect on any further beliefs not yet considered that may have been formed from your ancestral lineage. Consider the values, perspectives, and cultural norms that have been passed down through generations. Explore how these beliefs may have shaped your own worldview and influenced the way you navigate life. Are there beliefs that resonate with you and align with your authentic self? Conversely, are there any inherited beliefs that you find limiting or no longer serve your personal growth?

Write about the impact of these ancestral beliefs on your identity and how you can consciously choose which beliefs to embrace or release in order to align with your present understanding and aspirations.

ANCESTRAL INVOCATION

Before invoking your ancestors, consider setting up an ancestral altar or dedicating a space on your existing altar to your ancestors. Consider what symbols, objects, or mementos hold significance for honoring and connecting with your ancestral lineage.

My ancestral altar:

....

....

....

....

....

....

....

Follow the same ritual steps for the deity invocation in the previous section, except replace the deity invocation with an ancestor invocation.

Consider adding an additional beautiful step to your ancestral veneration: lighting three candles. Each one symbolizes a different aspect of time—the past, present, and future. They represent those who came before you, those with us now, and those who will follow in your footsteps.

On the next page is an example of an invocation. This particular one includes not only your own lineage but also honors the ancestors of the land where you live. It's a beautiful way to show respect for the sacred ground beneath your feet.

And finally, remember, ancestral veneration doesn't always need to be an elaborate formal event. It can be as straightforward as acknowledging their presence in your daily life or honoring the spirits of the land during your walks in nature.

Make this practice a regular part of your routine.

"I call upon the women and men from my mother's line.

I call upon the women and men from my father's line.

Lend me your strength, beauty, dreams, and joy –as I now
continue our lineage's work.

Infuse my life with energy and light so that I can transform my
wounds into healing, nurture hope, celebrate joy, and share love.

I am laying foundations and planting seeds for an abundant life
not only for myself but also for future generations.

Know that your lives were blessings; may you rest in peace
cradled by spirit. The light you carried lives on.

Ancestors, I honor you; I give thanks to you.

I seek your blessing–may your energy flow through me like a
sacred river coursing through my body and my life."

Begin the process of invoking your ancestors. Record your experiences and emotions during these sessions. Take note of any signs, sensations, or messages you may perceive. Reflect on the evolving connection between yourself and your ancestral spirits.

Embracing Cultural Practices

Are there cultural practices you would like to adopt and preserve as part of your ancestral heritage? Consider specific festivals, ceremonies, or rituals that hold significance for your cultural background.

How can you share these practices with others, especially younger generations, to ensure the preservation and continuation of your cultural heritage. What steps can you take to be a cultural steward and pass on these traditions for generations to come?

CONGRATULATIONS

Congratulations on completing this workbook in Kemetic spirituality. This experience has given you a glimpse into the rich fabric of this spiritual path, leading you through practices and contemplations that tie you to ancient wisdom. As you proceed, remember that Kemetic spirituality isn't just a list of rituals to complete—it's an ongoing spiritual development woven into your everyday life. Resist the urge to solely focus on "doing" and embrace the essence of "being." How can you embody the principles of Ma'at, honor your soul, relationships, deities, and ancestors in your everyday life?

This spiritual journey is more than just a lifelong commitment—it becomes part of who you are rather than something separate from your life. Take time to reflect on what you've learned from this workbook; let these experiences sink into your consciousness. Consider how you can authentically be in the world while staying attuned to your spiritual path and personal growth. Your connection with the deities, the concepts of Ma'at, and the guidance from your ancestors will continue to unfold and deepen over time.

I trust that this workbook has offered useful insights and practical tools for your path. If you feel moved to do so, please leave a review by scanning the QR code below. If you haven't already, consider delving into the accompanying book offering more resources and viewpoints on Kemetic spirituality. May your path be illuminated with wisdom, balance, and the enduring presence of the divine.

Book link:

FREE MEDITATIONS

Are you ready to elevate your spiritual journey and unlock the full potential of your inner self?

Deepen your transformation with our free meditations, carefully crafted to enhance and assist you on your spiritual journey.

Meditation 1:
Experience a blissful energetic healing of your heart, reconnecting you with your inner love and radiance, and opening yourself to more abundance in your life.

Meditation 2:
Explore the power of forgiveness with our Forgiveness meditation, where you will be guided through a sacred journey of emotional liberation. Release burdens, cultivate forgiveness, and experience the profound healing that comes from letting go.

Meditation 3:
Connect with your soul with our Higher-self meditation, unlocking inner wisdom, intuition, and spiritual insight.

These meditations, designed to accompany the workbook, serve as potent tools for transformation, healing, and spiritual growth.

Download your FREE meditations by scanning the QR code below:

Made in United States
Orlando, FL
19 November 2024

54125437R00072